A L[...]
MASS BOOK

THE ORDER OF MASS
The New Translation

All booklets are published thanks to the
generous support of the members of the
Catholic Truth Society

CATHOLIC TRUTH SOCIETY
PUBLISHERS TO THE HOLY SEE

CONTENTS

INTRODUCTORY RITES

The faithful establish communion and dispose themselves to celebrate the Eucharist worthily.

Before Mass begins, the people gather in a spirit of recollection, preparing for their participation in the Mass. All stand during the entrance procession.

Priest: In the name of the Father, and of the Son, and of the Holy Spirit.

Response: Amen.

The Priest greets the people with one of the following:

1. Pr. The grace of our Lord
Jesus Christ,
and the love of God,
and the communion
of the Holy Spirit
be with you all.

2. Pr. Grace to you and peace
from God our Father
and the Lord Jesus Christ.

3. Pr. The Lord be with you.

The people reply:

R. And with your spirit.

The Priest, or a Deacon, or another minister, may briefly introduce the faithful to the Mass of the day.

PENITENTIAL ACT

There are three forms of the Penitential Act which may be chosen from as appropriate. From time to time on Sundays, especially in Easter Time, instead of the customary Penitential Act, the blessing and sprinkling of water may take place as a reminder of Baptism. Each Penitential Act begins with the invitation to the faithful by the Priest:

Pr. Brethren (brothers and sisters), let us acknowledge our sins, and so prepare ourselves to celebrate the sacred mysteries.

A brief pause for silence follows. Then one of the following forms is used:

**1. I confess to almighty God
and to you,
my brothers and sisters,
that I have greatly sinned,
in my thoughts and in my words,
in what I have done
and in what I have failed to do,**

(*and, striking their breast, they say:*)

**through my fault,
through my fault,
through my most grievous fault;
therefore I ask blessed Mary
ever-Virgin,
all the Angels and Saints,**

and you, my brothers and sisters, to pray for me to the Lord our God.

---

2. Pr. Have mercy on us, O Lord.

R. For we have sinned against you.

Pr. Show us, O Lord, your mercy.

R. And grant us your salvation.

Invocations naming the gracious works of the Lord may be made, as in the example below:

3. Pr. You were sent to heal the contrite of heart:

Lord, have mercy.

Or: Kyrie, eleison.

R. Lord, have mercy.

Or: **Kyrie, eleison.**

Pr. You came to call sinners:
Christ, have mercy.
Or: Christe, eleison.

R. Christ, have mercy.
Or: **Christe, eleison.**
Pr. You are seated at the right hand
of the Father to intercede for us:
Lord, have mercy.
Or: Kyrie, eleison.

R. Lord, have mercy.
Or: **Kyrie, eleison.**

The absolution by the Priest follows:
Pr. May almighty God
have mercy on us,
forgive us our sins,
and bring us to everlasting life.
R. Amen.

The Kyrie, eleison *(*Lord, have mercy*) invocations follow, unless they have just occurred.*

Pr. Lord, have mercy.

R. Lord, have mercy.

Pr. Christ, have mercy.

R. Christ, have mercy.

Pr. Lord, have mercy.

R. Lord, have mercy.

Or:

Pr. Kyrie, eleison.

R. Kyrie, eleison.

Pr. Christe, eleison.

R. Christe, eleison.

Pr. Kyrie, eleison.

R. Kyrie, eleison.

The Gloria

On Sundays (outside of Advent and Lent), Solemnities and Feast Days, this hymn is either sung or said:

**Glory to God in the highest,
and on earth peace
to people of good will.**

**We praise you,
we bless you,
we adore you,
we glorify you,
we give you thanks
for your great glory,
Lord God, heavenly King,
O God, almighty Father.**

**Lord Jesus Christ,
Only Begotten Son,**

Lord God, Lamb of God,
Son of the Father,
you take away the sins of the
world, have mercy on us;
you take away the sins of the
world, receive our prayer;
you are seated at the right hand
of the Father, have mercy on us.

For you alone are the Holy One,
you alone are the Lord,
you alone are the Most High,
Jesus Christ,
with the Holy Spirit,
in the glory of God the Father.
Amen.

When this hymn is concluded, the Priest, says:

Pr. Let us pray.

And all pray in silence. Then the Priest says the Collect prayer, which ends:

R. Amen.

THE LITURGY OF THE WORD

By hearing the word proclaimed in worship, the faithful again enter into the unending dialogue with God.

First Reading

The reader goes to the ambo and proclaims the First Reading, while all sit and listen. The reader ends:

The word of the Lord.

R. Thanks be to God.

It is appropriate to have a brief time of quiet between readings as those present take the word of God to heart.

Psalm

The psalmist or cantor sings or says the Psalm, with the people making the response.

Second Reading

On Sundays and certain other days there is a second reading. It concludes with the same response as above.

Gospel

The assembly stands for the Gospel Acclamation. Except during Lent the Acclamation is:

R. Alleluia

During Lent the following forms are used:

R. Praise to you, O Christ, king of eternal glory! *Or:*

**R. Praise and honour to you,
Lord Jesus!** *Or:*

**R. Glory and praise to you,
O Christ!** *Or:*

**R. Glory to you, O Christ,
you are the Word of God!**

*At the ambo the Deacon, or the
Priest says:*

Pr. The Lord be with you.

R. And with your spirit.

Pr. A reading from the holy Gospel
according to *N.*

*He makes the Sign of the Cross
on the book and, together with the
people, on his forehead, lips, and
breast.*

R. Glory to you, O Lord.

At the end of the Gospel:

Pr. The Gospel of the Lord.

**R. Praise to you,
Lord Jesus Christ.**

After the Gospel all sit to listen to the homily.

The Homily

Then follows the Homily, which is preached by a Priest or Deacon on all Sundays and Holydays of Obligation. After a brief silence all stand.

The Creed

On Sundays and Solemnities, the Profession of Faith will follow. The Apostles' Creed may be used.

The Niceno-Constantinopolitan Creed

I believe in one God,
the Father almighty,
maker of heaven and earth,
of all things visible and invisible.

I believe in one Lord Jesus Christ,
the Only Begotten Son of God,
born of the Father before all ages.
God from God, Light from Light,
true God from true God,
begotten, not made,
consubstantial with the Father;
through him all things were made.

For us men and for our salvation
he came down from heaven,
(all bow)
and by the Holy Spirit was
incarnate of the Virgin Mary,
and became man.

For our sake he was crucified
under Pontius Pilate,
he suffered death and was buried,
and rose again on the third day
in accordance with the Scriptures.
He ascended into heaven
and is seated at the right hand
of the Father
He will come again in glory
to judge the living and the dead
and his kingdom will have no end.

I believe in the Holy Spirit,
the Lord, the giver of life,
who proceeds from the Father
and the Son,
who with the Father and the Son
is adored and glorified,
who has spoken through
the prophets.

I believe in one, holy, catholic
and apostolic Church.
I confess one Baptism
for the forgiveness of sins
and I look forward
to the resurrection of the dead
and the life of the world to come.
Amen.

The Apostles' Creed

**I believe in God,
the Father almighty
Creator of heaven and earth,
and in Jesus Christ,
his only Son, our Lord,**
(all bow)
**who was conceived
by the Holy Spirit,
born of the Virgin Mary,
suffered under Pontius Pilate,
was crucified, died
and was buried;
he descended into hell;
on the third day he rose again
from the dead;
he ascended into heaven,**

and is seated at the right hand
of God the Father almighty;
from there he will come to judge
the living and the dead.

I believe in the Holy Spirit,
the holy catholic Church,
the communion of saints,
the forgiveness of sins,
the resurrection of the body,
and life everlasting.
Amen.

The Prayer of the Faithful (Bidding Prayers)

Intentions will normally be for the Church; for the world; for those in particular need; and for the local community. After each there is time for silent prayer, followed by the next intention, or concluded with a sung phrase such as **Christ, hear us**, *or* **Christ graciously hear us**, *or by a responsory such as*:

Let us pray to the Lord.

R. Grant this, almighty God. *Or*:

R. Lord, have mercy. *Or*:

R. Kyrie, eleison.

The Priest concludes the Prayer with a collect.

THE LITURGY OF THE EUCHARIST

For Catholics, the Eucharist is the source and summit of the whole Christian life.

After the Liturgy of the Word, the people sit and the Offertory Chant begins. The faithful express their participation by making an offering, bringing forward bread and wine for the celebration of the Eucharist.

Preparatory Prayers

Standing at the altar, the Priest takes the paten with the bread and holds it slightly raised above the altar with both hands, saying:

Pr. Blessed are you,
Lord God of all creation,
for through your goodness
we have received
the bread we offer you:
fruit of the earth
and work of human hands,
it will become for us
the bread of life.

R. Blessed be God for ever.

*The Priest then takes the chalice
and holds it slightly raised above
the altar with both hands, saying*:

Pr. Blessed are you,
Lord God of all creation,
for through your goodness
we have received
the wine we offer you:

fruit of the vine
and work of human hands,
it will become our spiritual drink.

R. Blessed be God for ever.

*The Priest completes additional
personal preparatory rites, and the
people rise as he says:*

Pr. Pray, brethren
(brothers and sisters),
that my sacrifice and yours
may be acceptable to God,
the almighty Father.

**R. May the Lord accept
the sacrifice at your hands
for the praise and glory
of his name,
for our good
and the good of all his holy Church.**

The Prayer over the Offerings

The Priest says the Prayer over the Offerings, at the end of which the people acclaim: **R. Amen.**

The Eucharistic Prayer

Extending his hands, the Priest says:

Pr. The Lord be with you.

R. And with your spirit.

Pr. Lift up your hearts.

R. We lift them up to the Lord.

Pr. Let us give thanks
to the Lord our God.

R. It is right and just.

After the Preface all sing or say:

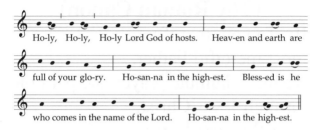

Ho-ly, Ho-ly, Ho-ly Lord God of hosts. Heav-en and earth are full of your glo-ry. Ho-san-na in the high-est. Bless-ed is he who comes in the name of the Lord. Ho-san-na in the high-est.

**Holy, Holy, Holy
Lord God of hosts.
Heaven and earth are full
of your glory.
Hosanna in the highest.
Blessed is he who comes
in the name of the Lord.
Hosanna in the highest.**

The congregation kneels.

Eucharistic Prayer I
(The Roman Canon)

Pr. To you, therefore,
most merciful Father,
we make humble prayer and petition
through Jesus Christ,
your Son, our Lord:
that you accept
and bless ✠ these gifts,
these offerings,
these holy and
unblemished sacrifices,
which we offer you firstly
for your holy catholic Church.
Be pleased to grant her peace,
to guard, unite and govern her
throughout the whole world,
together with your servant *N.*

our Pope and *N.* our Bishop,
and all those who,
holding to the truth,
hand on the catholic and
apostolic faith.

Remember, Lord, your servants
N. and *N.*
and all gathered here,
whose faith and devotion
are known to you.
For them, we offer you
this sacrifice of praise
or they offer it for themselves
and all who are dear to them:
for the redemption of their souls,
in hope of health and well-being,
and paying their homage to you,
the eternal God, living and true.

In communion with those
whose memory we venerate,
especially the glorious
ever-Virgin Mary,
Mother of our God and Lord,
Jesus Christ,
and blessed Joseph, her Spouse,
your blessed Apostles and Martyrs,
Peter and Paul, Andrew,
(James, John,
Thomas, James, Philip,
Bartholomew, Matthew,
Simon and Jude;
Linus, Cletus, Clement, Sixtus,
Cornelius, Cyprian,
Lawrence, Chrysogonus,
John and Paul,
Cosmas and Damian)
and all your Saints;

we ask that through
their merits and prayers,
in all things we may be defended
by your protecting help.
(Through Christ our Lord. Amen.)

Therefore, Lord, we pray:
graciously accept this oblation
of our service,
that of your whole family;
order our days in your peace,
and command that we be delivered
from eternal damnation
and counted among the flock of
those you have chosen.
(Through Christ our Lord. Amen.)

Be pleased, O God, we pray,
to bless, acknowledge,
and approve this offering

in every respect;
make it spiritual and acceptable,
so that it may become for us
the Body and Blood of your most
    beloved Son,
our Lord Jesus Christ.

On the day before he was to suffer,
he took bread in his holy
and venerable hands,
and with eyes raised to heaven
to you, O God, his almighty Father,
giving you thanks,
he said the blessing,
broke the bread
and gave it to his disciples, saying:

**'Take this, all of you, and eat of it,
for this is my Body,
which will be given up for you.'**

In a similar way,
when supper was ended,
he took this precious chalice
in his holy and venerable hands,
and once more giving you thanks,
he said the blessing
and gave the chalice
to his disciples, saying:

**'Take this, all of you,
and drink from it,
for this is the chalice of my Blood,
the Blood of the new
and eternal covenant,
which will be poured out
for you and for many
for the forgiveness of sins.
Do this in memory of me.'**

Pr. The mystery of faith.

The people continue, acclaiming one of the following:

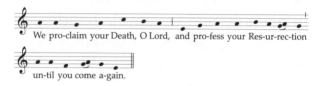

We pro-claim your Death, O Lord, and pro-fess your Res-ur-rec-tion
un-til you come a-gain.

**1. We proclaim your Death,
O Lord,
and profess your Resurrection
until you come again.**

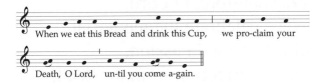

When we eat this Bread and drink this Cup,   we pro-claim your
Death, O Lord,   un-til you come a-gain.

2. When we eat this Bread and drink this Cup, we proclaim your Death, O Lord, until you come again.

Save us, Sav-iour of the world, for by your Cross and Res-ur-rec-tion
you have set us free.

3. Save us, Saviour of the world, for by your Cross and Resurrection you have set us free.

Pr. Therefore, O Lord,
as we celebrate the memorial
of the blessed Passion,
the Resurrection from the dead,
and the glorious Ascension
into heaven
of Christ, your Son, our Lord,
we, your servants
and your holy people,
offer to your glorious majesty
from the gifts that you have given us,
this pure victim,
this holy victim,
this spotless victim,
the holy Bread of eternal life
and the Chalice
of everlasting salvation.

Be pleased to look upon
these offerings
with a serene and
kindly countenance,
and to accept them,
as once you were pleased to accept
the gifts of your servant
Abel the just,
the sacrifice of Abraham,
our father in faith,
and the offering of your high priest
Melchizedek,
a holy sacrifice, a spotless victim.
In humble prayer we ask you,
almighty God:
command that these gifts be borne
by the hands of your holy Angel
to your altar on high
in the sight of your divine majesty,

so that all of us, who through this
participation at the altar
receive the most holy Body
and Blood of your Son,
may be filled with every grace
and heavenly blessing.
(Through Christ our Lord. Amen.)

Commemoration of the Dead

Remember also, Lord,
your servants *N.* and *N.*,
who have gone before us
with the sign of faith
and rest in the sleep of peace.
Grant them, O Lord, we pray,
and all who sleep in Christ,
a place of refreshment,
light and peace.
(Through Christ our Lord. Amen.)

To us, also, your servants,
who, though sinners,
hope in your abundant mercies,
graciously grant some share
and fellowship with your holy
Apostles and Martyrs:
with John the Baptist, Stephen,
Matthias, Barnabas,
(Ignatius, Alexander,
Marcellinus, Peter,
Felicity, Perpetua,
Agatha, Lucy,
Agnes, Cecilia, Anastasia)
and all your Saints;
admit us, we beseech you,
into their company,
not weighing our merits,
but granting us your pardon,
through Christ our Lord.

Through whom
you continue to make all these
good things, O Lord;
you sanctify them, fill them with life,
bless them, and bestow them
upon us.

*The Priest takes the chalice and the
paten with the host*:

Pr. Through him, and with him,
and in him,
O God, almighty Father,
in the unity of the Holy Spirit,
all glory and honour is yours,
for ever and ever.

R. Amen.

Then follows the Communion Rite,
page 71.

Eucharistic Prayer II

Pr. The Lord be with you.

R. And with your spirit.

Pr. Lift up your hearts.

R. We lift them up to the Lord.

Pr. Let us give thanks
to the Lord our God.

R. It is right and just.

Pr. It is truly right and just,
our duty and our salvation,
always and everywhere to give you
thanks, Father most holy,
through your beloved Son,
Jesus Christ,
your Word through whom
you made all things,

whom you sent as our Saviour
and Redeemer,
incarnate by the Holy Spirit
and born of the Virgin.

Fulfilling your will and gaining
for you a holy people,
he stretched out his hands
as he endured his Passion,
so as to break the bonds of death
and manifest the resurrection.

And so, with the Angels
and all the Saints
we declare your glory,
as with one voice we acclaim:

*The people sing or say aloud the
Sanctus as on page 27.*

Pr. You are indeed Holy, O Lord,
the fount of all holiness.
Make holy, therefore,
these gifts, we pray,
by sending down your Spirit
upon them like the dewfall,
so that they may become for us
the Body and ✠ Blood of our Lord
Jesus Christ.
At the time he was betrayed
and entered willingly into
his Passion,
he took bread and, giving thanks,
broke it,
and gave it to his disciples, saying:
'Take this, all of you, and eat of it,
for this is my Body,
which will be given up for you.'

In a similar way,
when supper was ended,
he took the chalice
and, once more giving thanks,
he gave it to his disciples, saying:
**'Take this, all of you,
and drink from it,
for this is the chalice of my Blood,
the Blood of the new
and eternal covenant,
which will be poured out
for you and for many
for the forgiveness of sins.
Do this in memory of me.'**

Pr. The mystery of faith.
*The people continue with the
acclamation as on page 34.*

Pr. Therefore, as we celebrate
the memorial of his Death
and Resurrection,
we offer you, Lord,
the Bread of life
and the Chalice of salvation,
giving thanks that you have
held us worthy
to be in your presence
and minister to you.

Humbly we pray
that, partaking of the Body
and Blood of Christ,
we may be gathered into one
by the Holy Spirit.

Remember, Lord, your Church,
spread throughout the world,

and bring her
to the fullness of charity,
together with *N.* our Pope
and *N.* our Bishop
and all the clergy.

---

*In Masses for the Dead, the following
may be added:*

Remember your servant *N.,*
whom you have called (today)
from this world to yourself.
Grant that he (she) who was united
with your Son in a death like his,
may also be one with him
in his Resurrection.

Remember also our
brothers and sisters
who have fallen asleep
in the hope of the resurrection,
and all who have died
in your mercy:
welcome them
into the light of your face.
Have mercy on us all, we pray,
that with the Blessed Virgin Mary,
Mother of God,
with the blessed Apostles,
and all the Saints who have pleased
you throughout the ages,
we may merit to be coheirs
to eternal life,
and may praise and glorify you
through your Son, Jesus Christ.

The Priest takes the chalice and the paten with the host:

Through him, and with him,
and in him,
O God, almighty Father,
in the unity of the Holy Spirit,
all glory and honour is yours,
for ever and ever.

R. Amen.

Then follows the Communion Rite, page 71.

Eucharistic Prayer III

Pr. You are indeed Holy, O Lord,
and all you have created
rightly gives you praise,
for through your Son our Lord
Jesus Christ,
by the power and working
of the Holy Spirit,
you give life to all things
and make them holy,
and you never cease to gather
a people to yourself,
so that from the rising of the sun
to its setting
a pure sacrifice may be offered
to your name.
Therefore, O Lord, we humbly
implore you:

by the same Spirit
graciously make holy
these gifts we have brought to you
for consecration,
that they may become
the Body and ✠ Blood
of your Son our Lord Jesus Christ,
at whose command
we celebrate these mysteries.
For on the night he was betrayed
he himself took bread,
and, giving you thanks,
he said the blessing,
broke the bread and gave it
to his disciples, saying:

'Take this, all of you, and eat of it,
for this is my Body,
which will be given up for you.'

In a similar way,
when supper was ended,
he took the chalice,
and, giving you thanks,
he said the blessing,
and gave the chalice
to his disciples, saying:
**'Take this, all of you,
and drink from it,
for this is the chalice of my Blood,
the Blood of the new
and eternal covenant,
which will be poured out
for you and for many
for the forgiveness of sins.
Do this in memory of me.'**

Pr. The mystery of faith.

The people continue with the acclamation as on page 34.

Pr. Therefore, O Lord,
as we celebrate the memorial
of the saving Passion of your Son,
his wondrous Resurrection
and Ascension into heaven,
and as we look forward
to his second coming,
we offer you in thanksgiving
this holy and living sacrifice.
Look, we pray, upon the oblation
of your Church
and, recognizing the sacrificial
Victim by whose death
you willed to reconcile us
to yourself,
grant that we, who are nourished

by the Body and Blood
of your Son
and filled with his Holy Spirit,
may become one body,
one spirit in Christ.
May he make of us
an eternal offering to you,
so that we may obtain
an inheritance with your elect,
especially with the most Blessed
Virgin Mary, Mother of God,
with your blessed Apostles
and glorious Martyrs
(with Saint *N.*: *the Saint of the day
or Patron Saint*)
and with all the Saints,
on whose constant intercession
in your presence

we rely for unfailing help.
May this Sacrifice
of our reconciliation,
we pray, O Lord,
advance the peace and salvation
of all the world.
Be pleased to confirm
in faith and charity
your pilgrim Church on earth,
with your servant *N.* our Pope
and *N.* our Bishop,
the Order of Bishops, all the clergy,
and the entire people
you have gained for your own.
Listen graciously to the prayers
of this family,
whom you have summoned
before you:

in your compassion,
O merciful Father,
gather to yourself all your children
scattered throughout the world.

† To our departed
brothers and sisters
and to all who were pleasing to you
at their passing from this life,
give kind admittance
to your kingdom.

There we hope to enjoy for ever
the fullness of your glory
through Christ our Lord,
through whom you bestow on
the world all that is good.†

The Priest takes the chalice and the paten with the host:

Through him, and with him,
and in him,
O God, almighty Father,
in the unity of the Holy Spirit,
all glory and honour is yours,
for ever and ever.

R. Amen.

Then follows the Communion Rite, page 71.

When this Eucharistic Prayer is used in Masses for the Dead, the following may be said:

† Remember your servant N.
whom you have called (today)
from this world to yourself.

Grant that he (she) who was united
with your Son in a death like his,
may also be one with him
in his Resurrection,
when from the earth
he will raise up in the flesh
those who have died,
and transform our lowly body
after the pattern of his own
glorious body.

To our departed brothers and
sisters, too,
and to all who were pleasing to you
at their passing from this life,
give kind admittance
to your kingdom.

There we hope to enjoy for ever
the fullness of your glory,
when you will wipe away
every tear from our eyes.
For seeing you, our God,
as you are,
we shall be like you for all the ages
and praise you without end,
(*He joins his hands.*)
through Christ our Lord,
through whom you bestow
on the world all that is good.†

Eucharistic Prayer IV

Pr. The Lord be with you.

R. And with your spirit.

Pr. Lift up your hearts.

R. We lift them up to the Lord.

Pr. Let us give thanks to the Lord our God.

R. It is right and just.

Pr. It is truly right
to give you thanks,
truly just to give you glory,
Father most holy,
for you are the one God
living and true,
existing before all ages
and abiding for all eternity,
dwelling in unapproachable light;

yet you, who alone are good,
the source of life,
have made all that is,
so that you might fill your creatures
with blessings
and bring joy to many of them
by the glory of your light.

And so, in your presence
are countless hosts of Angels,
who serve you day and night
and, gazing upon the glory
of your face,
glorify you without ceasing.
With them we, too,
confess your name in exultation,
giving voice to every creature
under heaven,
as we acclaim:

The people sing or say aloud the Sanctus as on page 27.

Pr. We give you praise,
Father most holy,
for you are great
and you have fashioned
all your works
in wisdom and in love.
You formed man in your own image
and entrusted the whole world
to his care,
so that in serving you alone,
the Creator,
he might have dominion
over all creatures.
And when through disobedience
he had lost your friendship,

you did not abandon him
to the domain of death.
For you came in mercy
to the aid of all,
so that those who seek
might find you.
Time and again you offered
them covenants
and through the prophets
taught them to look forward
to salvation.

And you so loved the world,
Father most holy,
that in the fullness of time
you sent your Only Begotten Son
to be our Saviour.
Made incarnate by the Holy Spirit
and born of the Virgin Mary,

he shared our human nature
in all things but sin.
To the poor he proclaimed
the good news of salvation,
to prisoners, freedom,
and to the sorrowful of heart, joy.
To accomplish your plan,
he gave himself up to death,
and, rising from the dead,
he destroyed death
and restored life.

And that we might live
no longer for ourselves
but for him who died
and rose again for us,
he sent the Holy Spirit
from you, Father,

as the first fruits for those
who believe,
so that, bringing to perfection
his work in the world,
he might sanctify creation
to the full.

Therefore, O Lord, we pray:
may this same Holy Spirit
graciously sanctify these offerings,
that they may become
the Body and ✠ Blood of our Lord
Jesus Christ
for the celebration
of this great mystery,
which he himself left us
as an eternal covenant.
For when the hour had come
for him to be glorified by you,

Father most holy,
having loved his own
who were in the world,
he loved them to the end:
and while they were at supper,
he took bread, blessed and broke it,
and gave it to his disciples, saying:

'Take this, all of you, and eat of it,
for this is my Body,
which will be given up for you.'

In a similar way,
taking the chalice
filled with the fruit of the vine,
he gave thanks,
and gave the chalice
to his disciples, saying:

**'Take this, all of you,
and drink from it,
for this is the chalice of my Blood,
the Blood of the new
and eternal covenant,
which will be poured out for you
and for many
for the forgiveness of sins.
Do this in memory of me.'**

Pr. The mystery of faith.

The people continue with the acclamation as on page 34.

Pr. Therefore, O Lord,
as we now celebrate
the memorial of our redemption,
we remember Christ's Death

and his descent
to the realm of the dead,
we proclaim his Resurrection
and his Ascension
to your right hand,
and, as we await
his coming in glory,
we offer you his Body and Blood,
the sacrifice acceptable to you
which brings salvation
to the whole world.

Look, O Lord, upon the Sacrifice
which you yourself have provided
for your Church,
and grant in your loving kindness
to all who partake of this
one Bread and one Chalice
that, gathered into one body

by the Holy Spirit,
they may truly become
a living sacrifice in Christ
to the praise of your glory.

Therefore, Lord, remember now
all for whom we offer this sacrifice:
especially your servant *N.* our Pope,
N. our Bishop,
and the whole Order of Bishops,
all the clergy,
those who take part in this offering,
those gathered here before you,
your entire people,
and all who seek you
with a sincere heart.

Remember also
those who have died in the peace
of your Christ

and all the dead,
whose faith you alone have known.
To all of us, your children,
grant, O merciful Father,
that we may enter
into a heavenly inheritance
with the Blessed Virgin Mary,
Mother of God,
and with your Apostles and Saints
in your kingdom.
There, with the whole of creation,
freed from the corruption
of sin and death,
may we glorify you
through Christ our Lord,
through whom you bestow.
on the world all that is good.

The Priest takes the chalice and the paten with the host:

Through him, and with him,
and in him,
O God, almighty Father,
in the unity of the Holy Spirit,
all glory and honour is yours,
for ever and ever.

R. Amen.

THE COMMUNION RITE

The eating and drinking together of the Lord's Body and Blood in a Paschal meal is the culmination of the Eucharist.

The Lord's Prayer

After the chalice and paten have been set down, the congregation stands and the Priest says:

Pr: At the Saviour's command and formed by divine teaching, we dare to say:

Together with the people, he continues:

Our Father, who art in heaven, hallowed be thy name;

**thy kingdom come,
thy will be done
on earth as it is in heaven.
Give us this day our daily bread,
and forgive us our trespasses,
as we forgive those
who trespass against us;
and lead us not into temptation,
but deliver us from evil.**

Pr. Deliver us, Lord, we pray,
from every evil,
graciously grant peace in our days,
that, by the help of your mercy,
we may be always free from sin
and safe from all distress,
as we await the blessed hope
and the coming of our Saviour,
Jesus Christ.

**R. For the kingdom,
the power and the glory are yours
now and for ever.**

The Peace

Pr. Lord Jesus Christ,
who said to your Apostles:
Peace I leave you,
my peace I give you;
look not on our sins,
but on the faith of your Church,
and graciously grant her
peace and unity
in accordance with your will.
Who live and reign for ever and ever.

R. Amen.

Pr. The peace of the Lord
be with you always.

R. And with your spirit.

Then the Deacon, or the Priest, adds:

Pr. Let us offer each other the sign of peace.

And all offer one another the customary sign of peace.

Breaking of the Bread

Then the Priest takes the host, breaks it over the paten, and places a small piece in the chalice, saying quietly:

Pr. May this mingling
of the Body and Blood
of our Lord Jesus Christ
bring eternal life to us
who receive it.

Meanwhile the following is sung or said:

**Lamb of God,
you take away the sins of the world,
have mercy on us.**

**Lamb of God,
you take away the sins of the world,
have mercy on us.**

**Lamb of God,
you take away the sins of the world,
grant us peace.**

Invitation to Communion

All kneel; The Priest genuflects, takes the host and, holding it slightly raised above the paten or above the chalice says aloud:

Pr. Behold the Lamb of God,
behold him who takes away
the sins of the world.
Blessed are those called
to the supper of the Lamb.

**R. Lord, I am not worthy
that you should enter
under my roof,
but only say the word
and my soul shall be healed.**

*While the Priest is receiving the
Body of Christ, the Communion
Chant begins.*

Communion Procession

After the priest has reverently consumed the Body and Blood of Christ he takes the paten or ciborium and approaches the communicants.

The Priest raises a host slightly and shows it to each of the communicants, saying:

Pr. The Body of Christ.

R. Amen.

When Communion is ministered from the chalice:

Pr. The Blood of Christ.

R. Amen.

After the distribution of Communion, if appropriate, a sacred silence may be observed for a while, or a psalm or other canticle of praise or a hymn may be sung. Then, the Priest says:

Prayer after Communion

Pr. Let us pray.
All stand and pray in silence for a while, unless silence has just been observed. Then the Priest says the Prayer after Communion, at the end of which the people acclaim:

R. Amen.

THE CONCLUDING RITES

The Mass closes sending the people forth to put what they have celebrated into effect in their daily lives.

Any brief announcements follow here. Then the dismissal takes place.

Pr. The Lord be with you.

R. And with your spirit.

The Priest blesses the people, saying:

Pr. May almighty God bless you, the Father, and the Son,
✠ and the Holy Spirit.

R. Amen.

Then the Deacon, or the Priest himself says the Dismissal:

Pr. Go forth, the Mass is ended. *Or*:

Pr. Go and announce the Gospel of the Lord. *Or*:

Pr. Go in peace, glorifying the Lord by your life. *Or*:

Pr. Go in peace.

To which the people respond:

R. Thanks be to God.

Then the Priest venerates the altar as at the beginning. After making a profound bow with the ministers, he withdraws.